GRAPHIC HEROES OF THE AMERICAN REVOLUTION

GEORGE WASHINGTON
AND THE WINTER AT VALLEY FORGE

BY GARY JEFFREY
ILLUSTRATED BY NICK SPENDER

Gareth Stevens
Publishing

Please visit our website, www.garethstevens.com.
For a free color catalog of all our high-quality books,
call toll free 1-800-542-2595 or fax 1-877-542-2596.

Library of Congress Cataloging-in-Publication Data

Jeffrey, Gary.
George Washington and the winter at Valley Forge / Gary Jeffrey.
p. cm. — (Graphic heroes of the American Revolution)
Includes index.
ISBN 978-1-4339-6014-7 (pbk.)
ISBN 978-1-4339-6015-4 (6-pack)
ISBN 978-1-4339-6174-8 (library binding)
1. Washington, George, 1732-1799—Headquarters—Pennsylvania—Valley
Forge—Juvenile literature. 2. Valley Forge (Pa.)—History—18th century—
Juvenile literature. 3. United States. Continental Army—Military life—
Juvenile literature. 4. Pennsylvania—History—Revolution, 1775-1783—
Juvenile literature. 5. United States—History—Revolution, 1775-1783—
Juvenile literature. I. Title.
E234.J44 2011
973.3'341—dc22
2010048672

First Edition

Published in 2012 by
Gareth Stevens Publishing
111 East 14th Street, Suite 349
New York, NY 10003

Copyright © 2012 David West Books

Designed by David West Books
Editor: Ronne Randall

Printed in China

CPSIA compliance information: Batch #DS11GS: For further information contact Gareth Stevens, New York, New York at 1-800-542-2595.

CONTENTS

RUNNING BATTLES

4

GEORGE WASHINGTON AND THE WINTER AT VALLEY FORGE

6

STAYING POWER

22

GLOSSARY

23

INDEX

24

In 1775, the thirteen American colonies formed a Continental army to fight against the British. General George Washington, a hero of the French and Indian War, was its commander in chief.

George Washington was forty-three years old when he became commander in chief.

A BORN LEADER

Washington was born and raised in Virginia as the son of a plantation owner. His father died when he was eleven, and young George quickly learned to rely on himself. A loyal British subject, he was honest, dependable, and brave in battle. His military service in the militia led him to become a member of the Continental Congress. He was an early supporter of the war.

Washington pictured crossing the Delaware in an early victory against the British.

VICTORIES AND DEFEATS

During the summer of 1777, the British attacked the patriots at Saratoga, on the Canadian border, and at Philadelphia, their capital. The Americans, under Washington, were forced to retreat from Philadelphia but won a great victory at Saratoga.

The patriot army was pushed hard during the Philadelphia Campaign.

Sir William Howe, the British commander in chief, took over Philadelphia.

The assault on Germantown cost the lives of many patriots.

DRIVEN BACK

Washington quickly struck back. He launched a bold attack on the British at Germantown, but was fought to a standoff. He had misjudged the abilities of his army.

GEORGE WASHINGTON
AND THE WINTER AT VALLEY FORGE

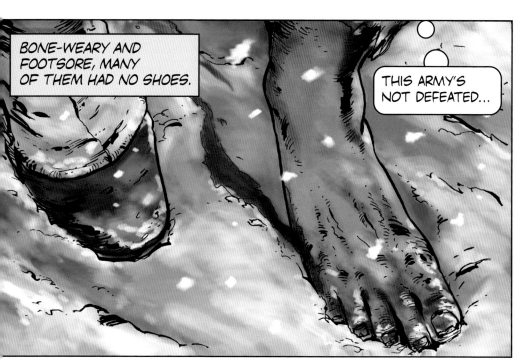

SUPPLIES SOON RAN LOW. ALL THE MEN HAD TO EAT WAS FLOUR MADE INTO...

...FIRECAKES! NOT AGAIN?!

BE GRATEFUL - IT'LL KEEP YOU ALIVE TO FIGHT AGAIN IN THE SPRING.

THE MEN WITHOUT SHIRTS OR BLANKETS HAD TO SLEEP CLOSE TO THE FIRE, SITTING UP.

THIS IS TERRIBLE - WE CAN'T LAST THE WHOLE WINTER LIKE THIS.

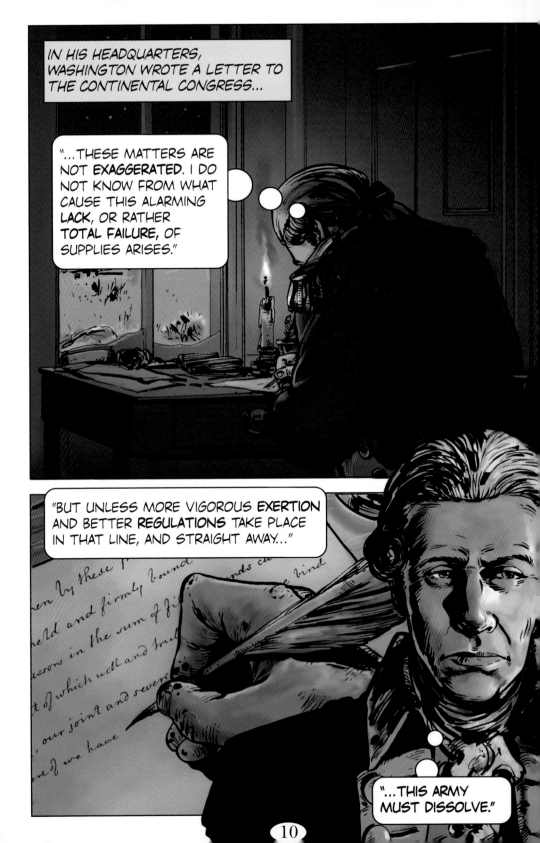

11

AS THE WEEKS WORE ON...

LACK OF STRAW TO SPREAD ON THE COLD GROUND IS MAKING THE MEN **SICK**.

OUR SOLDIERS ARE GOING TO DIE FOR WANT OF **STRAW**?

LOOK AT THE WRETCHES - THIS ISN'T AN ARMY, IT'S A MOB!

STILL THE SUPPLIES DID NOT COME...

CONGRESS HAS LITTLE FEELING FOR THE NAKED AND DISTRESSED SOLDIERS. I FEEL **GREATLY** FOR THEM, AND FROM MY SOUL I PITY THEM, WHOSE **MISERIES** I HAVE THE POWER NEITHER TO **RELIEVE NOR PREVENT**.

MEANWHILE, SIR WILLIAM HOWE, COMMANDER OF THE BRITISH FORCES, WAS ENJOYING ALL THAT PHILADELPHIA HAD TO OFFER.

SO, AM I RIGHT IN THINKING WE WILL NOT ATTACK THE CONTINENTALS THIS WINTER BECAUSE THEIR CAMP IS TOO WELL ENTRENCHED?

THAT'S RIGHT.

HEH, HEH, THERE YOU GO. ENGLISH GOLD - MUCH BETTER THAN WORTHLESS CONTINENTAL MONEY!

WE SHALL JUST LET THEM **SUFFER.** THEY WILL FIND NOTHING IN THE COUNTRYSIDE. OUR ARMY HAS PICKED IT CLEAN.

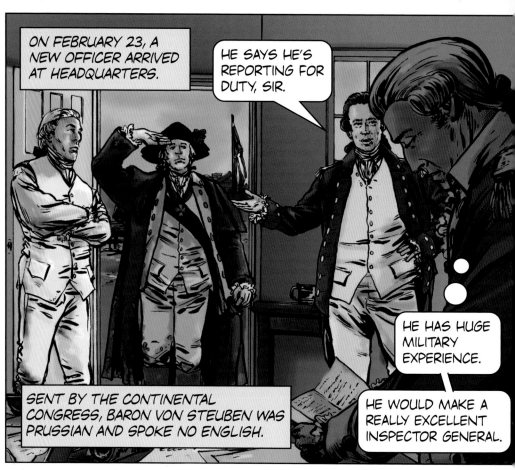

ON FEBRUARY 23, A NEW OFFICER ARRIVED AT HEADQUARTERS.

HE SAYS HE'S REPORTING FOR DUTY, SIR.

HE HAS HUGE MILITARY EXPERIENCE.

SENT BY THE CONTINENTAL CONGRESS, BARON VON STEUBEN WAS PRUSSIAN AND SPOKE NO ENGLISH.

HE WOULD MAKE A REALLY EXCELLENT INSPECTOR GENERAL.

VON STEUBEN LOOKED OVER THE CAMP...

HMMM... YOU INTEND TO MOVE THE KITCHENS AND LATRINES TO **OPPOSITE** SIDES OF THE CAMP.

SIMPLE GENIUS! WE WILL MAKE IT SO.

VALLEY FORGE WAS REORGANIZED ACCORDING TO VON STEUBEN'S PLAN.

SUPPLY PROBLEMS HAD BEEN EASED BY THE NEW QUARTERMASTER, NATHANAEL GREENE...

GO OUT OF STATE FOR HORSES, BUILD BRIDGES, MEND ROADS, CREATE ROUTES OF SUPPLY!

WE'VE GOT TO MAKE THIS ARMY FIT TO MOVE AT A MOMENT'S NOTICE.

ON MAY 3, THERE WAS GREAT NEWS.

THE FRENCH HAVE COME INTO THE WAR ON OUR SIDE!

STAYING POWER

The Battle of Monmouth was the last big battle in the north. The war lasted another five years, with defeats and victories on both sides, before the patriots won.

George Washington directs his commanders during the siege of Yorktown—the final, big British defeat.

END OF THE WAR

Washington had to endure a lack of supplies and money for his army, which led to mutinies. There were also betrayals and mistakes. By the time the war ended in 1783, Washington had grown old and gray.

FIRST PRESIDENT

At the end of the war, Washington resigned from the army. He refused to rule the nation as a military leader. Instead, he helped create the Constitution. In 1789, he was elected leader by the people and named president.

Washington lived until he was 67. He was made president twice.

GLOSSARY

amputation The cutting of a limb from the body.

betrayal Giving help or information to the enemy.

defensive Suitable place for defending and protecting.

drilling Training soldiers to march and use weapons.

endure To carry on and suffer without giving in.

entrenched A securely fixed position, usually in trenches.

exertion The act of making a huge physical effort.

forage To look for food and supplies.

frostbite Destruction of the skin and tissue as a result of exposure to freezing temperatures.

militia A group of citizens who are part of the military service.

mutiny A rebellion against the people or officers in charge.

patriot A person who supports and defends their country.

quagmire An area of soft, wet, boggy earth.

quartermaster An officer responsible for soldiers' food, clothing, and equipment.

standoff A tie or draw in a battle or competition.

INDEX

C
Congress, 4, 10, 12, 15–16
Continental army, 4, 14

D
Delaware, 4

F
French, 19–20
French and Indian War, 4

G
Germantown, 5
Greene, Nathanael, 19

H
Howe, Sir William, 5, 14

I
inspector general, 15–16

M
militia, 4
Monmouth, 21, 22

N
New York, 21

P
patriot army, 5, 22
Pennsylvania, 6
Philadelphia, 5, 8, 14, 20
Philadelphia Campaign, 5
president, 22

Q
quartermaster, 15, 19

R
recruits, 17

S
Saratoga, 5

seige of Yorktown, 22
standoff, 5
Steuben, Baron von, 16, 17, 18

V
Valley Forge, 6, 8, 15, 16, 20, 21